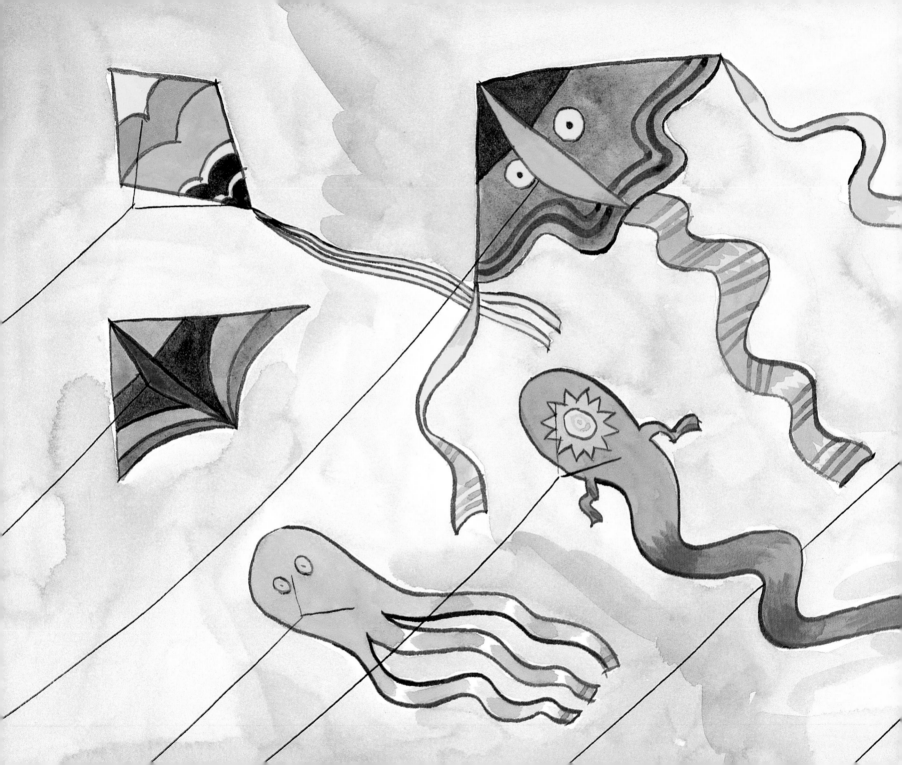

MathStart®
SYMMETRY

LET'S FLY A KITE

by Stuart J. Murphy • illustrated by Brian Floca

HarperCollinsPublishers

LEVEL
2

To the high-flying Edmond Murphy family—
Pat and Patty, Jan and Kraig, Barby, Suzi, and Jason
—S.J.M.

For Madeleine Strand
—B.F.

The publisher and author would like to thank teachers Patricia Chase,
Phyllis Goldman, and Patrick Hopfensperger for their help in
making the math in MathStart just right for kids.

The art for this book was created in ink line and watercolor.

HarperCollins®, 🔲®, and MathStart® are registered trademarks of HarperCollins Publishers.
For more information about the MathStart series, write to
HarperCollins Children's Books, 195 Broadway, New York, NY 10007.
or visit our web site at www.harperchildrens.com.

Bugs incorporated in the MathStart series design were painted by Jon Buller.

Let's Fly a Kite
Text copyright © 2000 by Stuart J. Murphy
Illustrations copyright © 2000 by Brian Floca

Library of Congress Cataloging-in-Publication Data
Murphy, Stuart J., date
   Let's fly a kite / by Stuart J. Murphy ; illustrated by Brian Floca.
      p.   cm. — (MathStart)
   "Level 2, symmetry."
   Summary: Two squabbling siblings learn about symmetry when their babysitter helps them build and fly a kite.
   ISBN 0-06-028034-4. — ISBN 0-06-028035-2 (lib. bdg.)
   ISBN 0-06-446737-6 (pbk.)
   I. Ratio and proportion—Juvenile literature.   2. Symmetry—Juvenile literature.
[1. Symmetry.   2. Kites.]   I. Floca, Brian, ill.   II. Title.   III. Series.
QA117.M88   2000   99-26550
512.9'24—dc21   CIP

Typography by Elynn Cohen
18 19 20 PC 21
❖

Ring! Ring! The doorbell rang one windy Saturday. Hannah and Bob raced to the door. There stood Laura, their favorite baby-sitter, with her dog, Ralph.

"Hi, kids," Laura said. "Anyone want to fly a kite today?"

"Yeah!" yelled Bob and Hannah.

"Okay, but we'll have to make one first," Laura said. Hannah and Bob watched as she cut a large diamond shape out of white paper.

They heard their parents open the back door. "We'll be back late this afternoon," called their dad. "Laura, there's a picnic basket on the kitchen counter."

"'Bye!" shouted Bob and Hannah together.

"Before we put this kite together, we have to decorate it. What do you think it should look like?" Laura asked.

"Let's decorate it with waves and whales," said Hannah.

"We should paint it red with a lightning bolt down the middle," said Bob.

"I know," said Laura. "I'll draw a line across the kite so you two can each have a part to decorate."

"The bottom part's bigger," said Bob. "I'll draw my lightning bolt there."

"Hey," cried Hannah, "that's not fair! Bob's part is bigger than mine."

"I have a better idea," said Laura. They watched as she erased the line and drew a new one. "If I draw the line down the middle, both sides are the same size and shape. Now, go to it!"

Markers, glitter, glue, and crayons flew everywhere. When they were done, Laura showed them where to put the supports and the string.

"Now who wants to try it out at the beach?" asked Laura.

"I do!" Bob shouted.

"Me too!" said Hannah.

Laura put the kite and picnic basket in the trunk of her car while Hannah and Bob climbed into the backseat. Ralph always got to sit in front. They were off to the beach!

"Bob, you're hogging the whole backseat," complained Hannah.

"Well, you were hogging it before," Bob replied.

"Hey, hey," said Laura, "there's enough room for both of you back there."

While they waited at a red light, Laura used her finger to draw an invisible line right down the middle of the seat. "Now both sides of the seat are exactly the same," she said. "And if I hear any more arguing back there, Ralph and I might eat the entire picnic ourselves!"

The rest of the ride was quiet. Before they knew it, they were at the beach.

"Who's hungry?" asked Laura as she took out the picnic basket.

"Me!" yelled Hannah.

"Me too!" said Bob. "I'm starving!"

"Well, at least you guys agree about *something*," said Laura. "I've got two picnic blankets here—one for Ralph and me, and one for the two of you. Why don't you go ahead and spread yours out?"

They unfolded their picnic blanket and Bob sat down.

"Hey, leave some room for me," cried Hannah.

"Here, I'll make a fold down the middle. Now both your sides are the same," said Laura, leaning over the blanket.

"Those sides look the same," said Bob, "but they're too skinny."

"What if I fold it like this?" said Laura. "The sides are the same this way too."

20

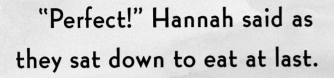
"Perfect!" Hannah said as
they sat down to eat at last.

21

Laura peeked back inside the picnic basket. "Looks like there's one banana-and-honey sandwich left," she said. "Who wants it?"

"Me!" shouted Bob.

"No, me!" shouted Hannah.

"Let's see," said Laura. "I'll cut it this way so you can share it."

"But that way the sides aren't the same shape and somebody gets a bigger piece," said Hannah.

"Okay, okay," said Laura. "How about this way, then?"

"Looks good," said Hannah.

"Tastes good too," added Bob.

When they were finished, Laura pulled the kite out of the trunk and shouted, "Let's fly a kite!"

"I want to fly it first," said Hannah.

"No way!" said Bob.

"You'll need to work together if you really want to make this kite fly," said Laura.

"Bob, you hold the kite high above your head and let go when I tell you," Laura instructed. "Hannah, you take the string, and when I say 'Run,' start running as fast as you can."

"I'm ready," said Hannah.

"Me too," said Bob.

"Run!" shouted Laura. "Bob, let go!" Ralph barked and raced Hannah down the beach. For a moment the kite hovered just above the ground.

"Let out more string, Hannah!" called Laura.

The kite started climbing high into the sky. But a few minutes later it suddenly dove toward the ground. "Go and help!" Laura shouted to Bob.

Bob caught up to Hannah, and she tossed him the string. They sprinted down the beach until the kite was flying high into the sky once more.

Bob and Hannah took turns making the kite swerve and dip. They even let Laura have a turn.

"You're a pretty good kite-flying team," Laura said.

Bob and Hannah grinned as they watched their kite soar far out over the ocean.

31

In *Let's Fly a Kite* the math concept is symmetry. Symmetry is a geometric property that helps us classify shapes. Examples of symmetry can be found everywhere: in nature, art, and architecture, and even in wallpaper patterns.

If you would like to have more fun with the math concepts presented in *Let's Fly a Kite*, here are a few suggestions.

- Read the story with the child and talk about the illustrations. Point out things like the kite and the sandwich that Bob and Hannah split between them and ask questions like: "If the kite is folded down the middle, will the two halves match exactly?"

- Look for symmetrical objects throughout the illustrations. See how many symmetrical objects you can find in the book.

- Make a snowflake by folding a square sheet of paper into fourths and cutting out small designs along the folds and edges. Find all the different ways the snowflake you made has symmetry.

- Together, look at things around your home that have symmetry: quilts, wallpaper, pieces of art.

Following are some activities that will help you extend the concepts presented in *Let's Fly a Kite* into a child's everyday life.

Nature Walk: As you walk through your neighborhood, look for all the things in nature that have symmetry: leaves, flowers, insects.

Symmetry Collage: Encourage your child to cut out pictures of symmetrical shapes from magazines. By folding the shapes or placing a small mirror on its edge across the middle of the shape, find and draw the line of symmetry on each.

My Closet: Have the child select various items of clothing that he or she thinks are symmetrical. Fold the clothes to check. Do any articles of clothing have more than one line of symmetry? Why do you think so many items of clothing are symmetrical?

The following books include some of the same concepts that are presented in *Let's Fly a Kite*:

- REFLECTIONS by Ann Jonas

- LAO LAO OF DRAGON MOUNTAIN by Margaret Bateson-Hill

- KITES by Demi

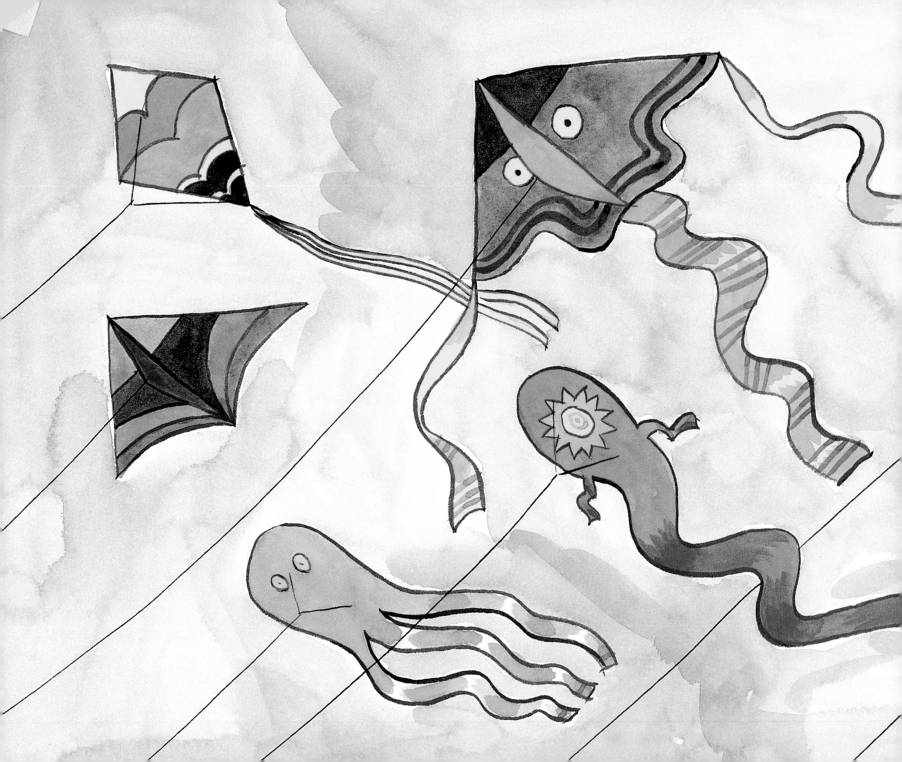